Railways & Recollections
1960

31624

Contents

First published in 2011

Cover photograph **READING:** Like so many other towns on the threshold of the Swinging Sixties, Reading in 1960 was a thriving railway centre. At lunchtime on Sunday 8 February photographer Ray Ruffell climbed the advanced starter signal gantry to capture this evocative scene as locomotive No 31851 pulls into the station with a passenger train that had left Redhill at 11.36am.

British Library Cataloguing in Publication Data
A catalogue record for this book is available from the British Library.

ISBN 978 1 85794 374 0

Silver Link Publishing Ltd
The Trundle
Ringstead Road
Great Addington
Kettering
Northants NN14 4BW

Tel/Fax: 01536 330588
email: sales@nostalgiacollection.com
Website: www.nostalgiacollection.com

Printed and bound in Česká Republika

Acknowledgements

First and foremost I would like to record our gratitude to the late Ray Ruffell, without whose efforts to photograph and record the railway scene in 1960 this book would not have been possible.

Frontispiece **REDHILL:** It's 21 March and driver Cyril White and his fireman pose for a photograph alongside 'U' Class No 31624 at Redhill after working the 12.05pm passenger service from Reading.

Introduction: Dawn of a new decade

The year 1960 brought with it new hope. After the austerity and rationing of the 1950s, Britain breathed a collective sigh of relief and the people let their hair down for what was to become known as the Swinging Sixties.

It was the start of a decade in which we would see the first man in space (1961), England win football's World Cup (1966) and the first men to walk on the Moon (1969). It was also the era of the most famous pop musicians of all time: The Beatles were formed in 1960 and disbanded in 1970.

On the railways, steam still reigned supreme, but the implementation of the Modernisation Plan of 1955 was starting to bite. Electric and diesel locomotives were appearing on our tracks in increasing numbers, yet the last steam engine, No 92220 *Evening Star*, didn't leave Swindon Works until 18 March 1960.

However, the spectre of the infamous Beeching Axe was in the near future and poised to fall like the Sword of Damocles; every railway user and enthusiast knew that the halcyon days of branch-line Britain were numbered.

Harold Macmillan was Prime Minister. Three years earlier, he'd famously told the British people that they'd never had it so good. Now, in 1960, he'd be making his most prophetic speech, telling South Africans that a 'wind of change' was blowing across their continent. In 1960 the glowing clamour for independence among African nations saw European colonial power slipping away.

Back home, 'Supermac' was probably right about never having it so good. The standard of living had been steadily rising through the 1950s and there was no reason to think that the new decade would be any different. Prosperity normally keeps politicians in power, but just around the corner a series of scandals would rock the Conservative administration in the early 1960s, as the spectre of sleaze figured in modern politics for the first time.

In 1960 the average house price was £2,530. A pint of beer cost 1s 7d (8p), a loaf of bread 1 shilling (5p), and a packet of 20 cigarettes would set you back just under 4 shillings (20p). There were only two TV channels – BBC and the fledgling ITV – but you could always go to watch a live football match…

It would cost you just half a crown (12.5p) to stand on the terraces at Old Trafford and see Bobby Charlton and his team mates play for Matt Busby's Manchester United. A season ticket would set you back about £8. Today it costs an adult £44 for a Man Utd home match roughly what their stars were paid each week back in 1960! Hooliganism and violence were virtually unheard of. Wooden rattles and knitted bobble hats ruled on the terraces.

To get to an away match, you'd almost certainly have climbed aboard a football special. Every available locomotive was pressed into service, some even hauled out of retirement, when the big cup finals were staged. The legions of travelling supporters wouldn't have gone by road, despite cheap fuel – 4-star petrol cost 4s 8d (24p) a gallon – because car ownership wasn't nearly so widespread and it took a long while to travel any distance by road. In 1960 the UK motorway 'network' consisted of the 8-mile M6 Preston bypass and a 67-mile stretch of the M1 that had been opened in November 1959 by the Minister of Transport, Ernest Marples.

The advent of the motorway age greatly pleased the scheming Marples. Prior to becoming a government minister he had owned one of the country's biggest road-building contractors. To avoid a 'conflict of interest', Marples had conveniently sold his shares in his company … to his wife!

Later in the decade, the reviled Dr Richard Beeching, Chairman of British Railways, would shoulder the blame for decimating the country's rail network, but it is often forgotten that he merely wrote the report. The real decision-maker at the time was his boss – you've guessed it – Ernest Marples.

As 1960 dawned, so Britain's beloved railway network – once the finest in the world – was about to be dismantled by the very man who stood to gain most by building the roads and motorways that would be needed to replace them. The politicians of the era could teach their modern counterparts a thing or two when it came to sleaze…

A decade later, and wanted for fraud, Marples fled the country in disgrace. He died in self-imposed exile in Monaco, in 1978.

But let's not allow the selfish actions of a few members of a decrepit government spoil our rosy-tinted view of a nation on the brink of an exciting new decade, of which our railways were still the very lifeblood. They were the fastest, most efficient form of public transport. The freight trains carried most of our food, fuel and furniture too – and that's just the stuff beginning with F.

In 1960 the railways kept lorries and cars off our streets and lanes. Children played in safety. Some say it was when Britain was at its very best, when we were at peace with ourselves as a nation.

Was it? We'll let you wallow in the nostalgia of this book and decide for yourselves…

REDHILL: The old railwayman was already a disappearing breed by 1960 – and railwayman/photographer Ray Ruffell recognised that. Ray was a fireman on British Railways' Southern Region, based at Reading, and also happened to be a keen photographer. He attempted to capture the real world of the footplate, with his colleagues often covered in soot, sweat and coal dust. For this photograph he was for once on the other side of the camera, pictured left with fellow fireman Knight from Tunbridge Wells West. It was taken on 23 March at Redhill, Surrey.

READING SOUTH MPD: Here's Ray again, this time on the footplate of 'U' Class 2-6-0 No 31614 at Reading South motive power depot.

READING: And again … this time on 'The Spur' at Reading with a dusting of January snow on the ground. The engine is 'N' Class 2-6-0 No 31871.

Below **READING:** Reading driver Bill Lund and Guildford guard Eddie Oxford confer before the departure of the 3.35pm passenger train to Redhill. The engine is 'V' Class No 30909 4-4-0 *St Paul's*.

The 'V' Class – also known as the 'Schools' Class – was a passenger locomotive designed by the Southern Railway's Chief Mechanical Engineer, Richard Maunsell, in 1930. It was later developed and improved by his successor, Oliver Bulleid, who fitted a multiple-jet blastpipe and a larger-diameter chimney in 1938. The locomotive pictured here was among this second batch.

Right **DEEPDENE:** It's driver Lund again, this time on the footplate of No 30906 *Sherbourne* – another 'V' Class 4-4-0, this time to the Maunsell specification – about to leave Deepdene on the 8.45am ex-Redhill to Reading.

REDHILL: It must have been the start of the shift on 3 May when spotlessly clean Reading fireman Derrick Allen posed for this picture alongside yet another 'V' Class 4-4-0, No 30914 *Eastbourne*, at Redhill.

REDHILL: Cleaner Tony James and shedman Bob Strange are dwarfed by the engine they're posing alongside on 17 February.

1960 Happenings (1)

January
- Aswan Dam construction begins in Egypt.
- A mine collapses at Coalbrook, South Africa, killing 500 miners.

February
- The first CERN particle accelerator becomes operational in Geneva, Switzerland.
- France tests its first atomic bomb – in the Sahara Desert of Algeria.

March
- Elvis Presley returns home from Germany, after being away on duty for two years.
- The United States military announces that 3,500 American soldiers will be sent to Vietnam.

April
- At the 32nd Academy Awards ceremony, *Ben-Hur* wins a record number of Oscars, including Best Picture.
- Elvis Presley records *Are You Lonesome Tonight?*

May
- Burnley Football club clinches First Division title; Wolves win the FA Cup.
- The US government approves the world's first contraceptive pill.

June
- New Zealand's first television station begins broadcasting.
- The BBC Television Centre opens in London.

READING SOUTH MPD: Coalman Bob Hill at Reading South with 'Q' Class 0-6-0 No 30540 and 'U' Class 2-6-0 No 31616, ready for action.

READING: Another photo taken on shed at Reading, this time with 'N' Class No 31864 and (left to right) shedman Bob Strange and drivers J. Rowe and F. Jarvis. The engine in the background is 'U' Class No 31616.

WINTER ON THE RAILS

The new year was less than two weeks old when Arctic-like blizzards swept across southern England. Happily there were no concerns about 'the wrong sort of snow' in those days, and the trains ran as normal.

In 1960, winter didn't bring the country to a standstill. Schools didn't close just because of a bit of snow, either. Back then, children still received free school milk – a small bottle every day containing a third of a pint for every pupil – which would invariably freeze solid in midwinter, with the expansion of the liquid lifting the silver foil cap off the top of the bottle. In my village school in Norfolk the crates of milk were placed close to the old pot-bellied iron stove to defrost in time for mid-morning break.

For the majority of schools there was no central heating. It was the same story at home, where open coal fires were the usual form of heating. In fact, coal was the driving force of the whole country. In 1960 the National Coal Board employed 634,000 miners (today, the biggest producer, UK Coal, employs just 2,900).

REDHILL: On the footplate of a steam locomotive in winter, the intense heat from the firebox was very welcome in the open cabs, which offered little shelter from the elements.

This photograph shows six-coupled 'Q1' No 33036 arriving at Redhill on the 10.10am freight from Tonbridge, where it was shedded together with 12 of its classmates. The austere lines of the 'Q1' made it look like a giant clockwork toy train – so much so that the legendary LMS locomotive designer Sir William Stanier, on seeing a 'Q1' for the first time, is reported to have asked, 'Where do you put the key?'

The 'Q1' was an austerity locomotive built by the Southern Railway during the Second World War. Designed by Oliver Bulleid, construction started at the SR's Brighton and Ashford works in 1942 and a total of 40 were built. It is widely considered to be the ultimate progression of the 0-6-0 steam engine, with unrivalled power in its class, and remained in service on Southern rails until 1966.

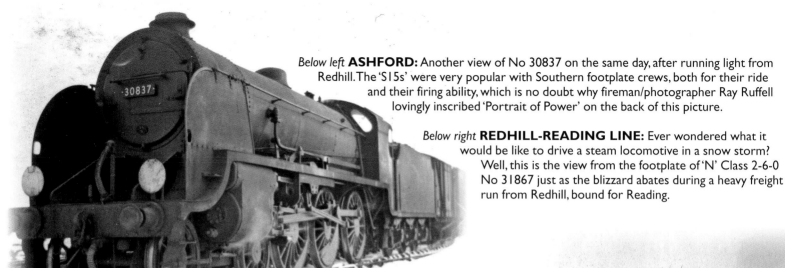

Below left **ASHFORD:** Another view of No 30837 on the same day, after running light from Redhill. The 'S15s' were very popular with Southern footplate crews, both for their ride and their firing ability, which is no doubt why fireman/photographer Ray Ruffell lovingly inscribed 'Portrait of Power' on the back of this picture.

Below right **REDHILL-READING LINE:** Ever wondered what it would be like to drive a steam locomotive in a snow storm? Well, this is the view from the footplate of 'N' Class 2-6-0 No 31867 just as the blizzard abates during a heavy freight run from Redhill, bound for Reading.

Above **ASHFORD:** Now here is a very special locomotive at work, in the yard at Ashford on 15 January, picking up freight for Reading. Why is it special? Because 'S15' No 30837 would become the last of its class to work on Southern lines, in 1966, when it would haul a 'Farewell to Steam' special train.

Forty-five Class 'S15' 4-6-0s were built, between 1920 and 1936 – initially by the London & South Western Railway, which was incorporated into the Southern Railway at the Grouping of 1923. The original design was by Robert Urie and it was continued, with modifications, by his successor, Richard Maunsell.

No 30837 was from the later batch ordered by Maunsell. Although it was the last to run for British Rail, this engine was not among the seven that were eventually saved for preservation – and which can now be seen variously on the Watercress Line, Bluebell Railway and the North Yorkshire Moors Railway, and other preserved lines from time to time.

THE FARNBOROUGH AIR SHOW

Today the Farnborough International Air Show is one of the most prestigious aviation events in the world, but back in 1960, when it was known simply as the Farnborough Air Show, it drew even bigger crowds. Every year, hundreds of thousands of people flocked to the Hampshire aerodrome to watch the fun – and most of them arrived by train, with specials running from all over the country.

The event had been staged at Farnborough since 1948. Early in its history, in 1952, the show had witnessed its biggest disaster when a de Havilland 110 broke up in the air, killing both crew members and 28 spectators on the ground, as well as injuring many more. These days such a tragedy would see the event curtailed and the venue closed – perhaps for weeks on end – while teams of crash investigators moved in to pick through the debris. But in those more stoical times, the show went on regardless, with pilots taking off from the wreckage-strewn runway to provide supersonic booms to the delight of the crowd.

Happily there were no crashes in 1960. The show opened each day with a Le Mans-style scramble of four huge V-bombers – mighty Valiants, Victors and Vulcans – simulating retaliatory strikes against an assumed communist aggressor. This was, after all, at the height of the Cold War!

The Farnborough Air Show was a great event for plane-spotters, but the Southern

metals around the area were a hotspot for trainspotters, too, for the duration of the show. Ray Ruffell made sure he had his trusty camera with him throughout the event to record the rare visitors to the region.

POLLOCK BRIDGE: In this photograph, taken at Pollock Bridge, Crowthorne, on Saturday 10 September, Great Western 2-6-0 No 5380 heads a 12-car relief express from Wolverhampton and Birmingham.

FARNBOROUGH LINE: On the same day, 'N' Class 2-6-0 No 31861 from Reading South hauls a six-coach shuttle service packed with people heading for the air show.

FARNBOROUGH LINE: Here 'U' Class 2-6-0 No 31625 pulls away from Sandhurst Halt with a six-coach stopping train.

LITTLE SANDHURST: Here's another 'U' Class 2-6-0, this time No 31798, passing Little Sandhurst at 60mph on a Western Region air show special from Cardiff to North Camp.

BRICKFIELD BRIDGE: An 'N' Class 2-6-0, No 31826, passes under Brickfield Bridge between Crowthorne and Sandhurst hauling another air show special from Reading South to North Camp.

LITTLE SANDHURST: Another locomotive a long way from home is ex-LNER 'B1' 4-6-0 No 61286 from Cambridge shed (31A), passing Little Sandhurst with yet another show special of 11 packed carriages. It had left its home in the East Anglian university city early on the morning of Sunday 11 September.

Designed for the LNER by Edward Thompson, 410 of these popular and powerful two-cylinder mixed-traffic locomotives were built between 1942 and 1948. The first 40 from the works at Darlington were named after species of antelope. No 8306 was named *Bongo*, which soon became the railwaymen's nickname for the entire class.

The 'B1s' operated throughout the LNER territory – initially on the former Great Eastern lines, where they hauled top-link expresses like the 'East Anglian', the 'Broadsman' and the 'Fenman' from London Liverpool Street to Ipswich, Norwich, Cambridge and King's Lynn. Later batches went to the Great Northern and Great Central areas.

The 'B1s' were urgently needed to rejuvenate the LNER's roster of elderly locomotives, but the new class didn't enjoy the longevity of its predecessors. No 61286 was among 150 'B1s' scrapped in 1962, less than two years after this photograph was taken.

SANDHURST HALT: GWR 2-6-0 No 6387 is checked at Sandhurst Halt while working a return air display special from new Camp to South Wales.

SANDHURST CUTTING:
Class S15 4-6-0 No 30837 passes Sandhurst Cutting en route to North Camp with an empty stock train to make up an air show special back to Reading.

SANDHURST HALT:
Reading driver Ward and fireman Nicklass are on the footplate of this 'N' Class 2-6-0, No 31401, pulling another six-car air show special to New Camp.

1960 Happenings (2)

July
- Harper Lee publishes her novel *To Kill a Mockingbird*, which wins the Pulitzer Prize.
- British yachtsman Francis Chichester crosses the Atlantic solo in a new record of 40 days.

August
- The newly formed Beatles begin a 48-night residency at the Indra Club in Hamburg, West Germany.
- The Soviet Union launches Sputnik 5, with two dogs, 40 mice and two rats on board. All survive.

September
- Cassius Clay wins the gold medal in light-heavyweight boxing at the Rome Olympic Games.
- *The Flintstones* debuts on TV.

October
- Nigeria becomes independent from the United Kingdom and becomes the 99th member of the United Nations.
- White South Africans vote to make the country a republic.

November
- Penguin Books is found not guilty of obscenity for publishing D. H. Lawrence's novel *Lady Chatterley's Lover*.
- John F. Kennedy is elected President of the United States – at 43 the youngest ever.

December
- The first episode of *Coronation Street* is screened. It had been planned to be a 16-part drama…
- The farthing, used since the 13th century, ceases to be legal tender in the United Kingdom.

Nr CROWTHORNE: Of course there was the usual scheduled passenger traffic during the air show weekend. Here's 'U' Class 2-6-0 No 31797 on a southbound Wolverhampton to Margate express, near Crowthorne.

SANDHURST HALT: 'Q' Class 0-6-0 No 30540 pulls away from Sandhurst Halt with the 5.31pm air show special from North Camp to Reading.

IT'S A DIRTY JOB...

Life on the footplate of a steam locomotive wasn't all glamour. it was cold in winter, blistering hot in summer, dirty and downright hard graft. But would those dedicated crews have had it any other way? Probably not!

Above **REDHILL:** Here is driver Arthur Neate in charge of 'S15' 4-6-0 No 30837 near Redhill motive power depot on 7 April. Note the giant coaler on the left of the photograph – these were once commonplace throughout the rail network. The three-road engine shed is to the right.

Top right **READING:** Taking water at Reading are driver Bill Lund in the foreground with his fireman keeping an eye on the tank of 'N' Class 2-6-0 No 31872.

Right **READING SOUTH:** Shedman Bob Hill is at work in the ash pits at Reading South. Loading one of the venerable seven-plank wooden coal wagons.

REDHILL MPD: One of the least-loved jobs in the engine shed was cleaning out the smokebox of a locomotive. This is Redhill motive power depot on 21 March, and the unidentified man inside the smokebox of 'Standard 4' 2-6-0 No 76054 is likely to be a fitter rather than an engine cleaner, as this engine together with 'S15' 4-6-0 No 30836 (left) and 'N' Class 2-6-0 No 31863 are all in dock for servicing or repairs.

Nr CHILWORTH: Although this photograph, taken on the evening of 16 April, is a little blurred – due to fireman Ray Ruffell balancing precariously on the tender to take it – we make no excuse for publishing it as it so eloquently captures the atmosphere as 'Q' Class 0-6-0 No 30549 storms the bank near Chilworth. Driver Vic Woodham is firing the engine during the photographer's absence from his duties!

1960 ARRIVALS AND DEPARTURES

ARRIVALS

Michael Stipe	American rock singer (REM)	4 January
Prince Andrew	Duke of York	21 March
Ayrton Senna	Brazilian racing driver (d1994)	19 February
Jeremy Clarkson	English journalist and television presenter	11 April
Bono	U2 singer	10 May
Mick Hucknall	English rock singer and songwriter (Simply Red)	8 June
Ian Hislop	British journalist and broadcaster	13 July
Sarah Brightman	English soprano and actress	14 August
Hugh Grant	English actor	9 September
Jean-Claude Van Damme	Belgian actor	18 October
Jonathan Ross	English television presenter	17 November
Carol Vorderman	British television presenter	24 December

DEPARTURES

Nevil Shute	English writer	12 January
Larry Marshall	Inventor of 'Velcro'	29 February
Eddie Cochran	American rock singer	17 April
Boris Pasternak	Russian writer, Nobel Prize laureate (declined)	30 May
Lottie Dod (88)	English tennis player, Wimbledon women's champion, 1887-88, 1891-93	27 June
Aneurin Bevan	Welsh politician	6 July
Sylvia Pankhurst	English suffragette	27 September
Clark Gable	American actor	16 November

Above **Nr CHILWORTH:** Driver Maurice Hockley keeps a watchful eye on the road ahead as 'U' Class 2-6-0 No 31623 rounds the curve about three-quarters of a mile east of Chilworth on the 5.47pm ex-Reading passenger train on 14 April.

I wonder if any of those passengers on that April evening looked out of the window of their carriage to witness the startling sight of their fireman wobbling atop the tender!

Right **REDHILL:** Another snapshot at Redhill finds fireman Ruffell on the other side of the camera. It's another 'S15' Class loco, this time No 30835.

Above **REDHILL MPD:** Here's No 31861 – another 'N' Class 2-6-0 – being prepared at Redhill motive power depot on 21 March.

Right **READING SOUTH MPD:** It's 5 February at Reading South and BR Standard Class 4 2-6-0 No 76055 is on the turntable, with fireman 'Romeo' Brown doing the pushing.

Right **REDHILL MPD:** It's the Redhill MPD turntable this time, on 3 May, with 'N' Class 2-6-0 No 31880.

Below **KESWICK:** Finally, in stark contrast to his toiling counterparts on the steam locomotives, here's the not-at-all-dirty driver of a diesel multiple unit (DMU) enjoying armchair comfort as he pulls away from Keswick, in Cumbria. Ray took this photograph on 23 August while on his summer holiday in Grange-over-Sands.

The DMU in question is No M79015, a two-car Derby Lightweight twin unit powered by two six-cylinder diesel engines, sending power to the wheels via a four-speed manual gearbox (unlike the bigger diesel locomotives of the day, which boasted huge diesel engines that drove

generators, in turn powering the electric traction motors on the axles). The Derby units were popular with drivers because of the panoramic view from the tall and distinctive front windows.

OSCAR WINNING PERFORMANCES 1960 ACADEMY AWARD WINNERS

Film: *Ben-Hur* wins a record 10 Academy Awards, including Best Picture, Best Director, Best Actor (Charlton Heston), Best Supporting Actor (Hugh Griffith), and Best Score.

Best Actress: Simone Signoret (*Room at the Top*)

Best Supporting Actress: Shelley Winters (*The Diary of Anne Frank*)

1960 No 1 Records

January
Adam Faith   *What Do You Wan*
Emile Ford & The Checkmates
                                        What Do You Want To Make
                                        Those Eyes At Me For
Michael Holliday   *Starry Eyed*
February
Anthony Newley   *Why*
March
Adam Faith   *Poor Me*
Johnny Preston   *Running Bear*
Lonnie Donegan   *My Old Man's A Dustman*
April
Anthony Newley   *Do You Mind*
May
Everly Brothers   *Cathy's Clown*
June
Eddie Cochran   *Three Steps To Heaven*
July
Jimmy Jones   *Good Timin'*
Cliff Richard   *Please Don't Tease*
August
Johnny Kidd & The Pirates   *Shakin' All Over*
The Shadows   *Apache*
September
Ricky Valence   *Tell Laura I Love Her*
October
Roy Orbison   *Only The Lonely*
November
Elvis Presley   *It's Now Or Never*
December
Cliff Richard   *I Love You*

SOUTHERN LINES

Right **CROWTHORNE:** Ray Ruffell worked on the footplate of locomotives on British Railways' Southern Region, so it's no surprise that there is a strong emphasis on his local lines in his photography. Nobody else captured the everyday workings of the area and era in such detail. For this photograph of No 31864 on a train from Reading powering out of Crowthorne with a fine exhaust, he got out of the cab and crouched at the lineside to get the right angle for a classic locomotive photograph.

Below left **SHOREHAM:** Here's a distinguished veteran – Class 'H' 0-4-4T No 31530 arrives at Shoreham with a local passenger service from Horsham.

The 'H' Class had a rich and fascinating career. Designed by Harry Wainwright for the South Eastern & Chatham Railway (SECR), 66 were built at Ashford Works between 1904 and the outbreak of the First World War in 1914 to work the SECR's suburban services out of London. With the Grouping of 1923 (when the SECR became part of the Southern Railway) and the electrification of many of the suburban lines from 1925 onwards, the small but powerful Class 'H' locomotives were dispersed further afield.

All but two survived into British Railways ownership in 1948, when they were converted to push-pull working on the quieter rural branch lines, like the one pictured. But with more and more of the Southern lines being electrified, the 'H' Class was living on borrowed time. Most were withdrawn by 1962, although a handful carried on working through to 1964 in Kent.

All were scrapped apart from one – No 31263, the last to be withdrawn, on 4 January 1964. It is now preserved on the Bluebell Railway in Sussex.

SOUTHAMPTON DOCKS: The duties of a Southern railwayman often took him into the heart of Southampton Docks where, on 3 August, Ray snapped this photograph of the great Cunard liner, RMS *Queen Elizabeth*, at berth.

At the time of her launch on 27 September 1938 she was the largest passenger liner of her day. She was named in honour of Queen Elizabeth, Queen Consort at the time and mother of our present monarch, later known as the much-loved Queen Mother, who passed away in 2002, aged 101.

In 1940 the great liner was pressed into service as a troopship, carrying 750,000 servicemen 500,000 miles during the war, before returning to civilian duties in October 1946, making transatlantic crossings in company with sister ship RMS *Queen Mary* between her home port and New York for more than 20 years.

Queen Elizabeth was retired from service in November 1968 and sold to a Hong Kong businessman who planned to turn her into a floating university. But while renovation work was taking place in 1972, she caught alight and capsized in Hong Kong harbour, after which she was scrapped.

READING MPD: Everybody makes mistakes – including railwaymen. On 19 April Ray was surprised to see these two Great Western 0-4-2T locomotives at the back of the engine shed at Reading. Both had arrived there in error … they were supposed to have gone to Swindon (No 1471) and Weymouth (No 1453). No explanation for their wanderings is given in Ray's photo notes.

For the record, the mislaid brace were both Class 1400 tank engines. Their home sheds were Exeter (1471) and Weymouth (1453).

READING MPD: This photograph taken from the footplate of 'N' Class 2-6-0 No 31826, and illustrates a typical busy railway scene in 1960. It is 16 February and 'Q' Class 0-6-0 No 30540 is on duty in the yard, while 'S15' 4-6-0 No 30837 stands on the bank with the 9.00am freight from Guildford. In the background an unidentified Great Western 'Castle'-hauled express blasts its way out towards London Paddington.

READING SOUTH BR 'Standard 4' 2-6-0 No 76054, in the charge of driver Gabriel of Redhill, leaves Reading South on Sunday 8 February with a mixed freight train bound for Redhill. The photographer climbed to the top of the down home signal gantry to capture this unique shot.

FREIGHT TRAINS

Freight was of secondary importance on the passenger-dominated Southern Railway until the outbreak of the Second World War. Suddenly, vast quantities of materials, weapons and vehicles needed to be transported to the South Coast, in the early years of the war in preparation for the expected invasion by Hitler's Nazis, and in the later years in readiness for the Allied invasion of Normandy in the opposite direction.

What passenger trains that did run were packed with military personnel. Every line was pressed into service – even the little 15-inch-gauge Romney, Hythe & Dymchurch Railway between Hythe and Dungeness, on the vulnerable Kent coast. The diminutive RH&DR had been conceived in the 1920s by two eccentrics – former army officer Captain J. E. P. Howey and Count Louis Zborowski, owner and driver of the original 'Chitty Chitty Bang Bang'. Both were millionaires, keen racing drivers … and miniature railway enthusiasts.

LITTLE SANDHURST: One engine that *did* haul plenty of the Southern Region's freight was the 'Q1', of course. With a tractive effort of 30,080lb, they were the most powerful 0-6-0 steam engines ever built and capable of pulling trains usually allocated to much bigger locomotives. Here 'Q1' No 33013 from Salisbury shed is pictured on 12 July near Little Sandhurst signal box at the head of a heavy mixed freight from Redhill.

Unfortunately the Count died while the scheme was still in its planning stages, but Captain Howey went ahead and opened the line on 16 July 1927. Originally it ran 8 miles from Romney to Hythe, but was later extended to Dungeness, 13.5 miles away.

It soon became famous as a tourist destination, billed as the 'Smallest Public Railway in the World'. But from 1939 to 1945 it became even better known after it was requisitioned by the War Department and ran the world's only miniature armoured train - leading to the rather bizarre sight of troops and guns crammed into tiny trucks and carriages and hauled by replica 'Pacific' locomotives in one-third scale, with drivers sitting astride the miniature tenders. It was a comical scene much loved by Pathé and other newsreel film-makers of the day, but it had a very serious purpose. At that time the Kent coastline was the part of Britain closest to Nazi-occupied Europe and invasion by Germany was a very real threat.

The urgent need for men and materials to be moved about along the South Coast saw a welcome investment in locomotives – especially freight engines like the powerful 'Q1' Class austerity 0-6-0 workhorses, designed by Southern's gifted CME, Oliver Bulleid.

But Bulleid was more than just a great constructor of modern locomotives: he also knew how to play the politics game. Besides needing freight locomotives, the Southern also urgently required new passenger engines, which Bulleid knew he would struggle to get approval to build during the war years. So,

rather disingenuously, he set about building two new 4-6-0 locomotives, which he designated as 'mixed traffic', which got round the wartime red tape.

The result was the successful 'Merchant Navy' Class 'Pacifics' and their lighter siblings, the 'West Country' Class. They were groundbreaking engines with modern innovations that included welded boilers, steel fireboxes and simplified servicing. Initially they were built with a streamlined casing, which earned them the nicknames 'Spam Cans', and which served little purpose other than to look good and attract favourable publicity. In later years it was removed.

Once the war was over, these three-

cylinder engines (including some of the later 'light Pacifics', which were known as the 'Battle of Britain' Class) were the mainstay of express passenger services throughout the region, right up to the end of steam. They even hauled a few freight trains, too…

SANDHURST CUTTING: Here's another typical mixed freight from 1960 – this time 'N' Class 2-6-0 No 31829 (from Bricklayers Arms shed) in Sandhurst cutting with a 16 November departure from Redhill.

CROWTHORNE: Invisible to the camera at the head of this 45-wagon mixed goods train is another class N mogul, No 31864 from Redhill shed, on the Dover-Reading heavy freight, on September 11. The photograph was taken near Crowthorne.

A total of 80 N class, plus six of the later three-cylinder N1s, were built by Richard Maunsell between 1917 and 1934, in three batches. Fifty were assembled from kits of parts made at the Royal Arsenal, Woolwich, earning them the nickname "Woolworths". They operated until the end of steam on Southern, in 1966. One survived into preservation – on the Watercress Line in Hampshire.

Bottom left **SANDHURST BRIDGE:** Reading goods guard Joe Paget leans from his brake-van as the 9.00am ex-Guildford freight passes below the soot-stained brickwork of Sandhurst Bridge.

Below **CROWTHORNE:** 'U' Class 0-6-0 No 31790 shunts in the goods yards at Crowthorne on 10 March.

READING SOUTH: This is what a busy goods yard looked like in 1960 – in this case Reading South loco shed and the up yard. Note the wide variety of rolling stock, with many of the wagons dating back to before the war.

CROWTHORNE: Standard Class 4 2-6-0 No 76053 is travelling tender first through Crowthorne station on 11 April because the Reading turntable is out of order. The modern BR design of the cab and tender make this a less unpleasant experience than it would have been on an older loco with a more exposed cab. No 76053 was the last of its class left at Redhill in 1960. A year earlier, ten had been stabled there.

The 2-6-0 Class 4 was designed by Robert Riddles and based on Henry Ivatt's LMS 2-6-0 design that had been built along austerity lines from 1947. There were 115 Class 4 locos built between December 1952 and November 1957. No 76053 is not among the four that survived into preservation – including one on Hampshire's Watercress line.

A HOLIDAY IN THE NORTH WEST

Lots of people go to Cumbria for their summer holidays. Most visit the Lake District National Park, but some head for the coast and resorts like Grange-over-Sands, which overlooks the sand and mud of Morecambe Bay. Among the latter was railwayman/photographer Ray Ruffell, but he wasn't armed with bucket and spade or knotted hanky. As always, he was more interested in the trains – particularly those hauled by ex-LMS locomotives that were either non-existent or rarities on his native Southern lines.

PRESTON: This is the sort of engine that Ray made the pilgrimage to the North West of England to see: ex-LMS 'Princess Royal' Class 'Pacific' No 46201 leaving Preston station on 25 August on the 11.10am express to Perth.

On the back of the print Ray describes the locomotive as *Princess Margaret*, but we're sure that's a case of mistaken identity because the number 46201 on the cabside is definitely that of her big sister, *Princess Elizabeth* (*Princess Margaret Rose* was No 46203).

A total of 13 'Princess Royals' were built at Crewe Works between 1933 and 1935. *Princess Elizabeth* was the second example of the class and named after the seven-year-old elder daughter of Albert, Duke of York (later King George VI). Today she is better known as HM Queen Elizabeth II!

The locomotive was withdrawn in 1962. Only two of the class were preserved – coincidentally *Princess Elizabeth*, at the Crewe Heritage Centre, and *Princess Margaret Rose* by the Princess Royal Locomotive Trust.

Tragically, one of the class, No 46202 *Princess Anne*, was among the locomotives involved in England's worst-ever railway disaster at Harrow & Wealdstone, eight years earlier on the foggy morning of 8 October 1952. She was double-heading a 15-vehicle express with 'Jubilee' Class 4-6-0 No 45637 *Windward Islands*, just 19 minutes into her journey from London Euston to Liverpool and Manchester and travelling at about 50mph, when the train ploughed into the wreckage of an earlier collision between a local stopping passenger train from Tring and the express sleeper train from Perth.

All six lines through the station were blocked by the wreckage, in which 112 people lost their lives and 340 were seriously wounded. Rescue work took several days, as 13 of the coaches had been squashed into a tangled heap of steel 45 yards long, 18 yards wide and 30 feet high.

The official report concluded that the driver of the Perth sleeper had missed a signal in the fog and ploughed into the back of the local service, setting in motion the tragic train of events. If the new Automatic Warning System (AWS) had been installed on the engine of the Perth express, the accident wouldn't have happened. This crash helped speed up the introduction of AWS throughout Britain's rail network.

Princess Anne was written off in the crash, although the name and number were later used on a short-lived experimental steam turbine locomotive. Remarkably, the battered engine of the sleeper, No 46242 *City of Glasgow*, was repairable, despite having taken the force of both collisions.

Right **GRANGE-OVER-SANDS:** Ray even chose a boarding house on Morecambe Bank Road where he could have a bedroom with a railway view. It was from that window on 28 August that he pictured this 'Black 5' 4-6-0 No 45233 at the head of one of the many seaside specials that were run in 1960.

Above **KESWICK:** Diesel multiple units (DMUs) were already operating many of the stopping services on the branch lines of Cumbria. On 23 August, on the former Cockermouth, Keswick & Penrith line, Ray took this view of Keswick station through the window of 150bhp Derby Lightweight two-car DMU No 79015.

BLACKBURN: On the same day, at Blackburn station, here's another elderly survivor – Midland 4-4-0 No 40684 on a three-coach local stopping service.

The LMS Class 2P was introduced back in 1928 and 138 were built at Derby between then and 1932, when this engine entered service. Its home shed in 1960 was Bank Hall, but its days were numbered: the last of the class were withdrawn in 1962, and all were scrapped.

It's a crying shame that such a ubiquitous engine that served light passenger services throughout the Midlands for so many years failed to make it into preservation, but it wasn't alone. Other famous classes that didn't get preserved include the big sister of the '2P', the 195-strong 4P LMS 'Compound' and the former Great Eastern Railway's legendary 'Claud Hamilton' Class 'D14/15/16'. To rub salt into the wounds of the railway enthusiast, all these engines were among the most celebrated 4-4-0s in the country – everyday engines that were a familiar sight throughout much of Britain.

That any locomotives at all were saved was down to the generosity and hard work of private individuals determined to save at least

some masterpieces of steam from oblivion. They got little encouragement from politicians.

Britain and its empire had been built on coal and steam. The nation owed a huge debt of gratitude to these machines, but the wrecking-ball attitudes of successive governments from the 1950s through to the 1960s were determined to sweep away all that heritage, without leaving a trace. A cynic would argue that politicians, with few exceptions, fail to appreciate both the relevance of the past and the legacy for the future. Quite some achievement when you come to think about it…

GRANGE-OVER-SANDS: Back off the hobbyhorse and on to Cumbrian lines, Stanier 'Black 5' 4-6-0 No 44987 approaches Grange-over-Sands with an express parcels train.

SEASCALE: Steaming through the dunes at Seascale is another 'Black 5', No 45230, on passenger duty with the 1.30pm Workington to Manchester train.

About a mile north of Seascale is Sellafield – the world's first nuclear power station – which began operating in the 1950s ... and was still hugely controversial when this photograph was taken, on 26 August 1960.

Left **SEASCALE:** Still in Seascale on the same day, here's a local stopping train from Barrow. The engine is once again a 'Black 5', this time No 45383, a Carlisle Kingmoor-based locomotive at the time.

Below **SEASCALE:** On that same 26 August yet another 'Black 5', No 45591, thunders past with a full load of furnace fuel.

Above **SEASCALE:** A storm was brewing – a common occurrence on the Cumbrian peninsula – when this photograph of Ivatt 4MT No 43026 heading a mineral train was taken at Seascale on 29 August.

Left **Nr SEASCALE:** Ex-LMS 4MT 2-6-4T No 42119 and Ivatt 4MT 2-6-0 No 43004 are the unusual combination double-heading this passenger service between Workington and Whitehaven on 27 August. Note how the curving track shadows the contours of the coast.

CARLISLE: Finally, on the way home to Southern rails on 31 August Ray was delighted to capture LMS 'Princess Royal' Class No 46203 about to leave for London. No identity hiccups this time – this is definitely *Princess Margaret Rose*.

STEAMING INTO THE SOUTH WEST

Much closer to Ray's Southern Region stamping ground was the South West peninsula – Cornwall, Devon and Somerset – and mainly Great Western territory, where he took these photographs.

LISKEARD: This is the Looe branch in Cornwall – a very significant line because it was one of those earmarked for closure by Dr Beeching in his report

The Reshaping of British Railways, yet was saved at the 11th hour in 1966. It is still open today, and more popular than ever, with passenger numbers growing by 14 per cent in recent years.

I wonder how many of those 4,000 miles of lines closed by BR in the wake of the Beeching Report would be successful today if only they had been spared the axe…

COOMBE JUNCTION: Another view of the Looe branch, and this time the locomotive is St Blazey-based '4500' Class 2-6-2T No 4565, a small 'Prairie' tank of which a total of 75 were built from 1906. The last ones were withdrawn in 1963 and no fewer than 14 were earmarked for preservation – examples can often be found on many of the preserved lines, including the Paignton & Dartmouth Steam Railway in Devon, the West Somerset Railway and the Severn Valley Railway.

Mechanical Engineer, Frederick Hawksworth. The final product was a free-steaming engine suitable for everything from freight to express passenger services to and from Paddington. All 30 survived into BR ownership before being scrapped in the 1960s.

County of Cornwall was built in 1945 and withdrawn in September 1963. None of the class survived into preservation, but a replica of No 1014 *County of Glamorgan* is under construction at Didcot Railway Centre.

ST ERTH: In this distant view of an unidentified express roaring past St Erth, the engine is another 'County' Class 4-6-0.

PENZANCE: What more appropriate engine could you hope to find simmering gently at Penzance station than GWR 'County' Class 4-6-0 No 1006 *County of Cornwall*?

Thirty of these engines, also known as the '1000' Class, were built at Swindon between 1945 and 1947, the result of a development project by the GWR's Chief

MINEHEAD: At Minehead station on 24 September GWR '5700' Class pannier tank 0-6-0PT No 7713 is waiting for passengers on the 4.30pm stopping service to Taunton.

The pannier tank was a mainstay of the GWR, following on from the similar saddle tanks that had been popular in the last three decades of the 19th century. An astonishing 863 of the '5700' Class were built between 1929 and 1950 – the majority (585) at GWR's Swindon Works, but others at W. G. Bagnall (100), North British Locomotive Co (75), and 25 each at Armstrong Whitworth, Beyer Peacock, Kerr Stuart and the Yorkshire Engine Co. Some 16 have been preserved.

ON SHED

While classic action photographs of steam engines blasting huge clouds of exhaust smoke and steam into a clear winter sky will always win the creative plaudits, the prosaic shots of lots of engines on shed are more likely to raise the temperature of the steam enthusiast.

The sight of these magnificent steam locomotives in one place, gathered like so many big game around a watering hole, will never be experienced in quite the same way again, so enjoy this selection from Ray's camera. Close your eyes and take a deep breath – you can almost smell the smoke and oil!

READING SOUTH MPD: Ray shinned up the advanced starter signal gantry at Reading South motive power depot on 8 February – a Sunday morning, when he was less likely to be spotted by disapproving superiors – to capture this historic view, with (left to right) 'Q1' 0-6-0 No 33007, BR Standard Class 5 4-6-0 No 73085, 'N' Class 2-6-0 Nos 31852, 31830 and 31867, and 'V' Class 4-4-0 No 30903.

READING SOUTH MPD: Steaming in unison on 17 February at Reading are 'S15s' Nos 30836 and 30847 and 'H15' No 30489.

GUILDFORD MPD: This is Guildford's roundhouse on 26 February. Locomotives present include Class 'M7' 0-4-4Ts Nos 30246 and 30132, diminutive 'B4' 0-4-0T No 30089 and a couple of unidentified Class 'U' 2-6-0s.

Below **REDHILL MPD:** BR 'Standard 4' 2-6-4 tank No 80031 is on the turntable at Redhill on 7 April. This most modern of tank engines was among 155 built by BR between 1951 and 1956 at Brighton, but based heavily upon an ex-LMS design from Fairburn ... which in turn was influenced by the Fowler tank engine of 1927. Perhaps not so modern after all.

Right **GUILDFORD MPD:** At Guildford shed on 26 February there's a truly veteran workhorse – Class 'B4' 0-4-0T No 30089, which was already more than 67 years old when this photograph was taken.

It was originally a dock shunter, one of 25 built to work at the big Southern docks like Southampton and Plymouth. No 30089 was originally named – *Trouville* – and first entered service in November 1892. It was scrapped in March 1963. Two of the class were preserved – one on the Bluebell Railway in Sussex and the other at Bressingham, Norfolk.

Above **READING SOUTH MPD:** Class 'L1' 4-4-0 No 31746 is pictured at the motive power depot on 18 February.

The 'L1' was Richard Maunsell's post-Grouping development of the 1941 'L1'. Introduced in 1926, some 15 of these high route availability (3P) passenger locomotives were built.

Right **READING SOUTH MPD:** An infrequent visitor to Reading South MPD was this 'H15' 4-6-0 heavy freight engine, No 30489, from Nine Elms. It was one of 26 designed by Robert Urie for the former London & South Western Railway, with 11 constructed in 1914 and another 15 from 1924 to 1925. They were employed at the head of fast, heavy freight trains throughout the Southern Railway area, but all were withdrawn and scrapped within a year of this photograph being taken, on 17 February.

Far right **READING SOUTH MPD:** Our final photograph from Reading shed was taken on 8 February and shows another rarity – a BR 'Standard 5' with a name. Some 172 of Robert Riddles's 5MT locomotives were build after nationalisation, between 1951 and 1957. None of them were named, apart from a batch of 20 that in 1959 received the names of a series of SR 'King Arthur' Class locos that had just been withdrawn. This is No 73085 *Melisande*, then shedded at Stewarts Lane.

Above **READING SOUTH MPD:** The low winter sun glints on these two engines at Reading shed on 5 February – 'U' Class 2-6-0 No 31614 and 'Q1' Class 0-6-0 No 33007.

Right **READING SOUTH MPD:** Imagine Ray Ruffell's excitement on 6 February when he was rostered to fire this beautiful veteran engine – Class 'C' 0-6-0 No 31723 – from Guildford to Reading, together with driver M. Nockley.

The 'C' Class was designed in 1900 by Harry Wainwright, Locomotive & Carriage Superintendent on the SECR. A total of 109 were built. All but two survived into BR ownership in 1948, but only a handful remained when this photograph was taken. All were scrapped apart from one, which can normally be found at the Bluebell Railway in Sussex.

AND FINALLY...

The year 1960 opened with Adam Faith at No 1 in the pop charts, singing *What Do You Want?*. If you'd asked that question of the huddle of young trainspotters shivering on the end of the station platform on 1 January they might have requested a duffel coat. Perhaps even a duffel bag. But what they really wanted most of all was more steam engines to tick off in their *ABC* books.

But as the new decade got under way, it was clear that steam's days were numbered. Exactly 12 years earlier, when the nation's railways were nationalised, the fledgling British Railways had inherited 20,000 locomotives of more than

440 types. Top of the new bosses' wish list was electric traction, followed by diesel, but post-war Britain couldn't afford either and built 12 types of standardised steam locomotives instead.

Coal was plentiful, the infrastructure was in place and the workforce knew steam. It seemed like steam was set to be around for a very long time, but progress marched on relentlessly and 1960 turned out to be a watershed year. March saw Swindon Works turn out Britain's last new steam locomotive, 9F No 92220 *Evening Star* ... yet over on the eastern side of the country steam power was disappearing fast.

Rural East Anglia and its quiet backwaters were losing money. Passenger numbers were

declining and freight services were light compared to the industrial areas of the country. A year earlier, the area had been the victim of the first axing of a main line – the Midland & Great Northern Joint Line from the East Midlands to Great Yarmouth. Many more were to follow later in the decade, but in the meantime diesel multiple units had temporarily breathed new life into the branch lines.

They were relatively fast and punctual and their quick turnaround meant that the frequency of most services doubled. They were clean, open and airy. Most passengers loved them.

Journey times were also being cut on the main lines – especially where Class 40 diesel-electrics had been introduced. On the main Great Eastern line from Liverpool Street to Ipswich and Norwich, they even surpassed the performances of the legendary 'Britannia' 'Pacific' steam engines.

By 1960, most of the steam services on BR's Eastern Region had been replaced by diesel power, but the new engines weren't bulletproof. The most reliable of the early engines was the Brush Type 2 (later Class 31), but even they were prone to teething problems – the most embarrassing of which came on 11 January when No D5667 broke down near Audley End while hauling the Royal Train to Norfolk, with HM The Queen on board. A rare lubricating pump failure was to blame, but BR took no more chances and future Royal Trains were double-headed by Class 31s.

Even in areas like the Midlands, where steam was strong, changes were clearly afoot. In January 1960 the British Transport Commission announced that it planned to demolish Euston station – including its magnificent 70-foot arch – as part of its scheme to electrify the West Coast Main Line. The destruction of the historic arch was fiercely contested by many famous figures, including the railway-loving poet, John Betjeman, but the only person who had the authority to step in refused to do so, on the grounds of costs £190,000 to save it compared to £12,000 to demolish it. His name? Transport Minister Ernest Marples.

The year 1960 ended with Cliff Richard topping the pop charts with the first of his many Christmas No 1s. The future looked bright for the young singer, but as Britain embarked on the adventure that would be known as the Swinging Sixties, we didn't know what to expect. Exciting times lay ahead, but steam fans knew they were heading for their final destination. Luckily fireman/photographer Ray Ruffell and his camera were ready to carry on snapping into the new decade, to capture that fading scene for posterity.

Index